GERARD TERBORCH DE OUDE

DUTCH MASTER DRAWINGS OF THE SEVENTEENTH CENTURY

SELECTED AND WITH AN INTRODUCTION

BY J. Q. VAN REGTEREN ALTENA

WITH 59 ILLUSTRATIONS

HARPER & BROTHERS · PUBLISHERS / NEW YORK

AUTHORIZED TRANSLATION

EDITIONS IN THE FRENCH AND GERMAN LANGUAGE
ARE PUBLISHED SIMULTANEOUSLY WITH THIS BOOK BY THE
HOLBEIN PUBLISHING COMPANY, BASLE

HELIOGRAVURE BY BÜCHLER & CO · BERNE
FOUR-COLOUR OFFSET PLATES MADE BY N. V. JOH. ENSCHEDÉ EN ZONEN, HAARLEM
AND PRINTED BY WASSERMANN AG., BASLE

1949

MASTER DRAWINGS

INTRODUCTION

If it is indeed a fact that the value of a work of art is to a certain extent qualified by the response of each new beholder, then the way we interpret it can hardly be a matter of indifference; we must keep an open and receptive mind. This applies even to the seemingly easily understood drawings created by the Dutch artists of the seventeenth century. For nearly three hundred years these treasures reposed between protective, white sheets in beautiful albums guarded within tooled leather bindings from the ravages of sun, dampness, and careless hands; today, in their unfaded freshness, they still convey to us the original ideas of the artists.

It is in the character of the drawing that the peculiar quality of these documents lies: in their lines, brush-strokes, and colours, we witness the process in the artist's mind by which a work of art is born. In a true sense, the preserved drawings are monologues by their creators, who experimented on these sheets, considered their next steps, and evaluated an effect they had striven to achieve. The studies by Rembrandt foreshadow the master's compositions before they were given mature form; figures to which he later gave final shape are here tentatively set forth. With a few strokes artists outlined groups of people or interiors, and indicated accessories so as to determine their just place within the general composition. Accents which must have seemed too strong have been dimmed with white body-colour, or an effect that seemed too uncompromising in the first sketch has been toned down. Then the ever-increasing knowledge of tone values, a knowledge enriched by each new experience, gradually led to a boldness and mastery which apparently was the more unconscious as the technical command of drawing was increased. The sensitive admirer of these drawings might well approach them with a certain diffidence; for through them he is admitted to the intimacy of the artist's first tentative thoughts and experiments. Possibly many of them were never intended for our eyes at all.

Ever since the sixteenth century, drawing had enjoyed a growing popularity. Even at an earlier date, a fully developed art of small drawings in silver-point or lead pencil had existed north of the Alps. It has been preserved in the form of single sheets—the few portrait studies by Jan van Eyck and his Flemish followers—or in still earlier sketchbooks, such as those in the Pierpont Morgan Library in New York and in the Pepysian Library of Magdalene College at Cambridge. These drawings are carried out in many different techniques and may be compared with those of the surviving North Italian sketchbooks. The passion for drawing, however, so characteristic of the

Florentine quattrocento, never reached the North. But it was in Italy that the earliest travellers systematically recorded their impressions in drawing; one of the most remarkable of these was Maerten van Heemskerck, the majority of whose sketches done on his journey to Rome (1532–1535) are preserved in the Kupferstichkabinett at Berlin. Those pages vividly reflect personal observations of Nature and, especially, of the works of art with which Rome was so richly endowed. It was, then, not until the sixteenth century that the Northern artist began to work with the quick stroke of a supple hand. At any rate, this is the assumption so long as we find no such sketches by Rogier van der Weyden, whose journey to Italy took place in 1449.

If, therefore, at the end of the sixteenth century, and even at the beginning of the seventeenth, we encounter small drawings carried out with silver-point on a carefully prepared yellow or yellowish-brown ground or priming, we may be sure that we are here dealing with the last exponents of this old technique: to this category belong the unique series of small masterpieces by Hendrick Goltzius (Plates 1, 7b), preserved for the most part in the Teyler Museum at Haarlem; the perhaps still more accomplished series by the best of his pupils, Jacques de Gheyn (Plate 7a); and, finally, the charming portrait announcing Rembrandt's engagement to Saskia (Plate 6). Briefly written notes are often added, such as we find in the sketches by earlier artists.

Goltzius' activity as a draughtsman occurs chiefly before 1600. Yet he lived to see the development of the new artistic tendencies of the seventeenth century; indeed, he anticipated its achievements in some of his studies (Plate 1), which surprise us with their realism, now free from the somewhat pedantic and manneristic pleasure in elegantly curved lines that characterized his earlier work. His Dutch landscapes of 1603 and 1604 are the first drawings of their kind (Plate 2); he was the first to discover the charm of the wide plains at the foot of the dunes of the "Kennemerland."

The restraint from exaggerated and ornate presentation was the essential progress made by some of the contemporaries of Goltzius: by Abraham Bloemaert who, until his death in 1650, at almost ninety years of age, preserved, even in the representation of the most commonplace subjects, the graceful line based on the study of the Italian eclectics (Plate 3); and by Jacques de Gheyn who must be credited with an innate feeling for the perfect drawing, virtuosity and a creative imagination (Plates 4, 5, 7a).

Yet even greater realists, foregoing all whims of personal interpretation, were the Dutch painters of everyday life: among these were the painter of architecture, Pieter Saenredam, the cripple, who knew as no other how to render the play of light and shadow on stone buildings and whitewashed walls (Plate 11); the painter of winter, Hendrick Avercamp, the mute, who took as much pleasure in bright colours, as in the delicate reflections of wintry skies on icy surfaces (Plate 8); and finally, the painter of the world of elegance and fashion, Willem Buytewech, the Witty—a title given him during his lifetime—whose mastery was unobtrusive beneath the facile touch of his quill-pen, as in the drawing of an empty room (Plate 12), which, had it been enlivened by a human figure, could have been recognized with greater certainty as the work of his hand.

To reproduce Nature, exactly as they saw it, to pass nothing by without drawing it, gradually became such an obsession that the training of a young artist required much patient study of drawing. In the Terborch family at Zwolle, the enlightened father began early to set an example to his children (Frontispiece); a considerable number of the sketches done by several of them in their youth are preserved in the Rijks-Prentenkabinet at Amsterdam. The father supervised these attempts, dated them, and recorded the progress made. He doubtless promoted the development of his son Gerard by sending him to the old artistic centre of Haarlem as a pupil of Pieter de Molijn; but before the young Gerard could draw his accomplished views of the Market at Haarlem (Plate 13), he must have made many thorough detail-studies in the quiet of his own country home.

As the taste for drawing increased, even among amateurs, artists began to specialize. At first they were fascinated by landscapes, but soon some of them did not find enough satisfaction in the Dutch scene. For others its simple, charming vistas held lasting attraction. Van Goyen and De Vlieger wandered or sailed along the rivers of Holland, where a lively picture always meets the eye. There are the groups of trees and their reflections in the slowly flowing water, the huts and castle ruins, the little walled towns, and the ever-changing skies above. All this we can rediscover in hundreds of small sketches lightly done in pencil and brush (Plates 14, 15) as well as in two sketchbooks by Van Goyen, which are still intact in private collections.

For many, on the other hand, Italy had lost nothing of her attraction, but artists now saw the country in a new light. The classic art of the Antique and the Renaissance, for all the charm it still exerted, took second place to Nature. Buildings, formerly the object of antiquarian curiosity, had to harmonize with the landscape, and nothing seems to have stimulated the artist's ambition more than the attempt to render accurately the play of light on leaves and the surfaces of walls. Certainly the sunny, bright skies of Italy were more favourable to these aims than those at home; in Holland, the artist was only just beginning to discover the impressive, translucent character of large clouds and moist atmosphere. Such untiring studies, some painstakingly executed, others only slightly sketched, created the basis for a new optical knowledge.

The great masters, however, went their own way. Apart from those of Rembrandt, not many of their drawings are known to us. Only a few rare, undisputably authentic examples by Jan Steen, Frans Hals and Jan Vermeer can be found. In order to understand this fact, it may be more illuminating to forego a general explanation and to seek individual answers in the work of each of these artists. Jan Steen, for example, is neither more painter nor less draughtsman than Aelbert Cuyp, and yet a great number of Cuyp's drawings have come down to us. Frans Hals was so spontaneous an artist, that all preliminary drawing must have seemed an unnecessary step to him in the preparation of a picture. With Vermeer, on the other hand, we may sooner assume an opposite temperament which inclined him to create his works in long hours of deep contemplation. Thus, all that can be established is that some artists were great draughtsmen without being great painters, and again, that with many painters we do not possess the material to follow in drawings the development of their works.

In the abundance of his production, Adriaen van Ostade came nearest to Rembrandt. Though distinctly talented as a painter, even in his most fruitful years he did not neglect his etching work and continued drawing in various styles until late in life. At first he favoured a rapid sketch, cursory yet containing the germ of the final effect; but, with the inner peace which came to him later, the Brouwer-like passion which at first had enlivened his landscapes and interiors seems to subside. The drawing begun as a sketch often served as a study for a carefully finished water-colour, which, in turn, could become the preparatory stage of a painting. The colouring of these aquarelles, despite its richness, is not nearly as brilliant as that of Avercamp but, softly subdued, it blends into a harmonious whole (Plates 34, 35).

It is interesting to observe how Rembrandt's development, with respect to technique, does not differ essentially from that of Van Ostade, even though it was governed by other laws. The effect of colour, comparatively rare in his early work and inseparable from a strongly marked chiaroscuro (Plate 18), later gains in importance, despite the continuing monochrome. From a drawing draughtsman Rembrandt progresses to become a painting draughtsman, a development not confined to this artist alone. Especially during his first ten years in Amsterdam, he must have filled his sketchbooks with studies of all the people around him (Plate 20). Thereafter, he turned to drawing landscape motifs to which, with his sure sense of composition, he gave a monumental quality that far surpassed the importance of the particular subject (Plate 22). With the ever-increasing mastery of his material, Rembrandt's once purely objective representations were imperceptibly enhanced by his personal interpretation.

It is to be regretted that there exist no preparatory studies for *Dr. Tulp's Anatomy Lesson* and *The Night Watch*. Could it be that Rembrandt deliberately destroyed all that might have diminished the magical effect of these two masterpieces? This same question presents itself with regard to other famous seventeenth-century paintings: Paul Potter's *Bull;* his equestrian portrait, as well as those by Rembrandt; the series of great portrait groups by Frans Hals; Terborch's memorial painting of the *Peace of Westphalia* and his *Magistrates of Deventer;* the principal works of Vermeer and Steen, and Van Goyen's marvellous views of the Valkhof at Nijmegen.

In contrast, a wealth of surviving material enables us to participate in the long hours of study in Rembrandt's studio, where Van den Eeckhout, Maes and Bol learnt to draw from the model and were taught to bring their studies to the level of perfection of small masterpieces (Plates 30, 31). Such drawings are in contradistinction to the studies of the genre painters whose figures make no pretence of having other than transitional function and ought to be considered in relation to the composition in which they werę to be included (Plates 38, 41, 42, 51). When these figures were repeated or varied in pose on the same sheet (Plate 51), it is their grouping especially, that makes for the charm of the page. A certain aesthetic calculation gradually becomes unmistakable in these juxtapositions (Plate 42). A taste for such calculated effects was fashionable at the time, and becomes more and more marked as intuitive creation yielded to conscious skill. Caspar Netscher was already carrying out his small pictures in brushwork that rivalled that of the Japanese, and his technique allows of no improvement (Plate 47). Aert van der Neer still captures a moonlit scene in unstudied grandeur (Plate 36), but Nicolaes Berchem has a more artificial approach; his pastoral scene depicts a deliberate pose rather than a chance situation (Plate 37). An idealized light unmodulated by atmospheric conditions, now brings everything into clear, plastic relief. This constituted a striving toward abstraction along the lines of the classical ideal, which artists had formerly tried so hard to overcome.

Nevertheless, the second half of the seventeenth century, which brought forth much attractive talent, still holds numerous charming finds. Jan de Bisschop and the young Constantin Huygens who tried their hands at drawing for their own pleasure, proved their talent in small-scale drawings, remarkable for their exact observation and lively representation of subject (Plates 54, 55). In this manner, Huygens, who accompanied Prince William III on his military campaigns, drew a kind of diary; as his written notebooks, corresponding with it, have also been preserved, we are able to follow exactly the artist's way and activities. His work must have been well known to the etcher Seymour Haden, for Haden's touch reminds one as much of these drawings as of Rembrandt's etchings.

Numerous, too, are the artists who devoted time and patience to the representation of flowers, animals, and detail studies of natural objects. Agneta Block, a passionate cultivator of flowers and plants—the first person who succeeded in raising pineapples in Holland—invited well-known draughtsmen to work at her country place on the river Vecht. By the end of her life, this famous lady possessed albums of drawings by Withoos, Herman Saftleven, Bronckhorst, and others, illustrating every flower which bloomed at "Vijerhof" (Plate 56).

This is not the only instance in which the works of artists have been of value as factual records. It is to the studies Roelant Roghman made about 1644 of a series of castles near Utrecht, that we are indebted for our presice knowledge of those structures. The superb drawings by Lambert Doomer enable us to trace the route of his journey down the Rhine as far as Switzerland, and back through France (Plate 29). To make his book on fire engines more comprehensible, Jan van der Heyden could have found no better solution than he did in illustrating it himself (Plate 51). And could we not find many other books which would scarcely retain our interest today were it not for their beautiful illustrations engraved after drawings?

Indeed, when we look over all these portraits, the views of towns and houses, the pictures of historical scenes—especially those of naval battles—and of curious natural phenomena at home or abroad, the thought readily suggests itself that the cultural history of seventeenth-century Holland is here portrayed, no less adequately than in words, in this faithful chronicle consisting of an almost limitless wealth of drawings.

After Rembrandt's death it became apparent that artists in their concentration on an exact rendering of their subjects fell short, not, indeed, in virtuosity, but in artistic sensibility. That which the great masters in their wise restraint had left to the spectator's imagination, was now laid bare and thrust into harsh focus.

In the second half of the century there was, however, one artist who, working on his own, set himself a higher aim: to give expression to the power, the greatness and the mystery of Nature. Like Hercules Seghers and like Rembrandt, Jacob van Ruisdael is a lonely figure; like them, he stands detached against a background of fluctuating artistic tendencies and performances. From the shadowy depths of his drawings an unobtrusive figure barely emerges here and there, while old oaks and graves seem to reflect the artist's meditations on his own transitoriness (Plate 48). Nothing theatrical or trivial can hold him. His brush does reproduce a tree leaf by leaf, but every detail contributes to the composite effect suggesting an imminent thunderstorm. Ruisdael's activity does but postpone the threatened artistic decline already becoming manifest; this great artist persuades us to believe for a moment in the continuance of an epoch which in fact was coming to an end.

Yet the rich harvest of the seventeenth century remains an important part of our cultural heritage. And though these drawings are often but the blossoms without which the fruit could not ripen, they possess on this account no less charm and character; they retain to this day, fresh and magical, the creative spark of the great masters.

NOTES ON THE PLATES

GERARD TERBORCH THE ELDER

Born at Zwolle in 1584; died there in 1662

Terborch the Elder may be considered a true lover of the art of drawing. He lived a quiet life in the little town of Zwolle in Gelderland, where from 1621 on he held the post of tax-collector. He made the traditional journey to Rome in 1602. Most of the drawings he made there are distinctive because of their originality rather than their artistic qualities.

Frontispiece — GIRL READING

Pen, with grey and brown wash, and red chalk. 97×89 mm. $3^7/_8 \times 3^1/_2$ in.
Amsterdam, Rijks-Prentenkabinet.

Possibly the portrait of his daughter Gesina.

HENDRICK GOLTZIUS

Born at Mühlbracht, Jülich, in 1558; died at Haarlem in 1617

The best known engraver of his time; also a good draughtsman and painter. Began his career as a painter of small portraits and later became the leader of the so-called "Mannerist" school of Holland. His journey to Rome in 1590 and his studies of Antique art inclined him temporarily to almost pure Classicism, but he finally found his way back to Realism. As in the case of Dürer, his numerous drawings—the most beautiful are in the Teyler Museum in Haarlem—enable us to follow closely the versatile development of his style.

1 — GIRL READING A BOOK

Signed with the monogram HG and dated 1605. Black and red chalk. 260×192 mm.
$10^1/_4 \times 7^1/_2$ in. Berlin, Kupferstichkabinett.

2 — DUNES NEAR HAARLEM

Signed with the monogram HG and dated 1603. Pen. 87×153 mm. $3^3/_8 \times 6$ in.
Rotterdam, Boymans Museum.

The selection of these two drawings does not take into account Goltzius' abundant production previous to 1600. Both are specimens of the artist's later style.

ABRAHAM BLOEMAERT

Born at Gorkum in 1564; died at Utrecht in 1651

Painter of historical subjects, portraits, and landscapes. Studied for a time in Paris. Although an eclectic, he never completely lost his original delight in classical forms. He contributed to the education of the younger generation of artists by publishing, for their use, a collection of engravings on various themes.

3 COURTYARD OF A DUTCH HOUSE

Pen, wash and water-colour. 164×217 mm. $6^1/_2 \times 8^1/_2$ in. Leyden, Prentenkabinet.

Though not an early work, this study still has a purely graphic character. It was used as the study for the left side of a painting by the master, which is now in the Engleson Collection at Malmö. A later water-colour in the Brussels Museum presents, in turn, a variation of the left side of the drawing. It is surprising to find the artist, whose inspiration was usually drawn from the classic deities of Olympus, here choosing a subject which paves the way for Pieter de Hooch.

JACQUES DE GHEYN

Born at Antwerp in 1565; died at The Hague in 1629

Engraver, draughtsman, and subsequently painter. Pupil of Goltzius, whom in the extreme exactitude of his small portraits he almost surpasses. He seems to have attached an even greater importance to drawing than did his master, and he worked out an entirely individual style for himself, which found few imitators, though it may have influenced Rembrandt in his early period.

4 TREES IN THE WIND

Pen on grey paper. 288×206 mm. $11^3/_8 \times 8^1/_8$ in. Amsterdam, Rijks-Prentenkabinet.

One of the numerous sheets that give evidence of the artist's nature studies; trees, especially, interested him.

5 A BOY AND HIS MOTHER LOOKING AT A PICTURE-BOOK

Pen and wash. 147×147 mm. $5^3/_4 \times 5^3/_4$ in. Berlin, Kupferstichkabinett.

Probably De Gheyn has here portrayed his wife and his only son, who later became a painter too. If this is so, the drawing must date from about 1599, not long before his wife's premature death.

REMBRANDT VAN RIJN

Born at Leyden in 1606; died at Amsterdam in 1669

The great painter of biblical and historical subjects, of portraits and landscapes, lived from about 1631 in Amsterdam. His etched work comprises around three hundred plates. His drawings are even more numerous; they are distinguished by the variety of subject matter, the sureness with which effects are calculated; of special interest is the recurrent treatment of identical themes at various stages of the artist's development.

6 PORTRAIT OF HIS BETROTHED, SASKIA

Silver-point on vellum. 185×107 mm. $7^1/_4 \times 4^1/_4$ in. Arched top.
Berlin, Kupferstichkabinett.

The drawing has the following inscription: "*dit is naer mijn huysvrou geconterfeyt, do sij 21 jaer oud was den derden dach als wij getroudt waeren—den 8 Junijus 1633*" (this is drawn after my wife, when she was 21 years old, the third day after we were betrothed, June 8, 1633).

JACQUES DE GHEYN

(For biographical note see page XIV)

7a PORTRAIT OF A MAN OF QUALITY

Oval miniature, adapted for a box-lid. Lead pencil on yellow primed paper. 65×55 mm. 2 5/8×2 1/8 in. Groningen, Gemeente Museum.

A small portrait, similar in manner to those which we see in the engravings of Goltzius and De Gheyn, and which they would also draw simply with the lead pencil.

HENDRICK GOLTZIUS

(For biographical note see page XIII)

7b SITTING DOG

Lead pencil on prepared paper. 100×73 mm. 4×2 7/8 in. Amsterdam, Fodor Museum.

The back of this sheet shows further sketches: a leg of the same dog, and a sleeve. The dog appears again in a drawing showing Adam and Eve in Paradise (Kunsthalle, Hamburg).

HENDRICK AVERCAMP

Born at Amsterdam in 1585; died at Kampen in 1635

Painter of landscapes and especially winter scenes, a charming artist who in his drawings and water-colours skilfully portrayed the life of his time. A fine series of his drawings is in the Rijks-Prentenkabinet at Amsterdam; the Royal Library at Windsor contains the leaves of a sketchbook by his hand.

8 A FOWLER ON THE ICE

Signed with the monogram HA. Water-colour. 152×192 mm. 6×7 1/2 in. Amsterdam, Rijks-Prentenkabinet.

This drawing led to a painting which is now in a Dutch private collection.

9 SOWING SEED NEAR A COUNTRY HOUSE

Signed with the monogram HA (entwined). Chalk and water-colour. 131×191 mm. 5 1/8×7 1/2 in. Amsterdam, Rijks-Prentenkabinet.

This delightful reminiscence of seedtime was probably inspired by the country near the river Yssel.

ROELANT SAVERY

Born at Courtrai in 1576; died at Utrecht in 1639

Painter of landscapes, often with numerous animals. During his work at the court of Rudolph II at Prague, Savery probably became familiar with mountain scenery of which he made frequent use in his sketches. Later, when he was living in Holland, he used the sketches again for the composition of his pictures.

10 STUDY OF A FIR

Signed with the monogram RS. Black and red chalk, retouched with the pen and heightened with white. 376×151 mm. $14^3/_4$×6 in. Berlin, Kupferstichkabinett.

Savery, who inherited Brueghel's vision, discovered new motifs in the mountainous scenery of which both artists were so fond.

PIETER SAENREDAM

Born at Assendelft in 1597; died at Haarlem in 1665

Painter of architecture. His works are essential documents for the study of the Gothic architecture of the Netherlands. His drawings, with notes in his own hand, were preparatory studies for his paintings. Taken as a series they constitute documentary evidence of the highest importance.

11 THE TOWER OF UTRECHT CATHEDRAL

Pen and water-colour. 510×383 mm. $20^1/_8$×$15^1/_8$ in. Utrecht, Gemeente-Archief. Inscribed: "Pieter Saenredam fecit. Int. jaer 1636 den 15 October deze binnen Utrecht volteykent" (Pieter Saenredam finished this on the 15th October 1636 at Utrecht).

During his stay in Utrecht in 1636, Pieter Saenredam tirelessly devoted himself to drawing the old churches in that town. Some of the drawings were used as a basis for paintings, but we know of no further variation of the sketch here described.

WILLEM BUYTEWECH (?)

Born at Rotterdam in 1585; died there in 1625 or 1627

Etcher and genre painter; known as "*geestige Willem*,"—"witty William." This nickname seems extraordinarily appropriate, in view of the piquant way and free style with which this sharply observant artist captures the character of his period in his pictures. In this respect his work has a certain affinity with Rembrandt in his early period.

12 INTERIOR OF A PRINCE'S CHAMBER

Crayon, pen and wash. 197×326 mm. $7^3/_4$×$12^7/_8$ in. Amsterdam, Rijks-Prentenkabinet.

The attribution is tentative, since it would involve dating the drawing before 1627. But though its authorship may be disputed, this drawing undoubtedly displays the spirit of Buytewech. The name of Adriaen van de Venne, to whom it was hitherto attributed, cannot be definitely discounted.

GERARD TERBORCH THE YOUNGER

Born at Zwolle in 1617; died at Deventer in 1681

Painter of portraits and genre subjects of great distinction. His fame was definitely established from the time when he painted the *Peacemakers of Munster*, as single portraits and as a group (London, National Gallery). His career included journeys to Rome and to Madrid. The majority of his drawings, including the earliest studies, as well as drawings by several members of his family, are in the Rijks-Prentenkabinet at Amsterdam.

13 THE MARKET AT HAARLEM

Black chalk and wash. 185×295 mm. 7 1/4×11 5/8 in. Haarlem, Teyler Museum.

At the farthest end of the market place is the Town Hall, ancient residence of the Counts of Holland, and its scaffold.

JAN VAN GOYEN

Born at Leyden in 1596; died at The Hague in 1656

Landscape painter. Pupil of Esaias van de Velde. The astonishing ease of Van Goyen's brushwork is already noticeable in his drawings, which consist of innumerable variations on nature motifs. He was particularly successful in rendering sunlit effects on the banks of Dutch rivers, with soft transitions from light to shadow.

14 HOUSES ALONG THE RIVER

Signed with the monogram IVG and dated 1652. Black chalk and wash. 115×200 mm. 4 1/2×7 7/8 in. Amsterdam, A. Welcker Collection.

One is tempted to remark that drawings like those of Van Goyen contain the germ of a method of handling later brought to full fruition by the Impressionists.

SIMON DE VLIEGER

Born at Rotterdam in 1600; died at Weesp in 1653

Landscape painter. Influenced by Van Goyen and Rembrandt. He was one of the artists who developed the painting of atmosphere, of light and air. His drawings are by no means rare, but not all are equally good.

15 SAILING SHIPS IN DUTCH WATERS

Signed with the monogram S de V (pricked for transfer). Black chalk and wash. 158×266 mm. 6 1/4×10 1/2 in. Amsterdam, Rijks-Prentenkabinet.

FRANS HALS

Born at Antwerp about 1580; died at Haarlem in 1666

Portrait painter; leader of the Haarlem School. Apparently he seldom made preparatory sketches for his canvases; his drawings are therefore very rare.

16 PORTRAIT OF A NOBLEMAN IN A BROAD-BRIMMED HAT

Black and white chalk on blue paper. 194×152 mm. 7 5/8×6 in. London, British Museum.

Study for a portrait now in the Hermitage, Leningrad, in which the hat has been overpainted. As the hat had been part of the original conception, the authorship of the drawing is proved. The portrait belongs to the master's second period.

CORNELIS VISSCHER

Born probably at Haarlem in 1619, or 1629; died at Haarlem in 1662

Engraved portraits and a few genre pictures. His drawings, which also are mostly portraits, are distinguished by a keen observation, reminiscent of Frans Hals.

17a STUDY OF A SKULL

Black chalk. 94×113 mm. $3^3/_4 \times 4^1/_2$ in. Amsterdam, Rijks-Prentenkabinet.

Another drawing of a skull by this artist is in the same collection. Such studies served painters as accessories in their still-life pictures, or with portraits, to suggest the transience of life.

BARTHOLOMEUS BREENBERGH

Born at Deventer in 1599, or 1600; died at Amsterdam about 1658

Painter, chiefly of landscapes and mythological scenes. During his long stay in Rome, he was particularly fascinated by landscapes with classical remains. He was one of the first to capture successfully the sun-drenched atmosphere of the South.

17b CORSICA AND THE SATYR

Signed: BB (entwined) f. 164· Red chalk and bistre wash. 78×119 mm. $3^1/_8 \times 4^3/_4$ in. Amsterdam, Rijks-Prentenkabinet.

The scene is in the style of the small pictures by Adam Elsheimer, who died in 1610, with which Breenbergh may have become acquainted in Rome. The subject is inspired by the *Pastor Fido* of Guarini.

REMBRANDT VAN RIJN

(For biographical note see page XIV)

18 CHRIST AND THE DISCIPLES

Signed: Rembrandt f. 1634. Black and red chalk, pen, and water-colour heightened with gouache. 350×476 mm. $13^3/_4 \times 18^3/_4$ in. Haarlem, Teyler Museum.

One of Rembrandt's rare drawings in colour, exceptional also because of its large size.

19 FIGURES IN CANDLELIGHT

Brush-drawing. 175×190 mm. $6^7/_8 \times 7^1/_2$ in. Bayonne, Musée Bonnat.

It is not impossible that this drawing represents Saskia. It is tempting to compare it with the etching (Bartsch 367), taking into account the inversion due to printing. However, it cannot be proved that this is a study for the etching, neither can we tell whether the central figure is the young bridegroom observing the scene in a mirror, nor whether a female figure is intended. There are other possible interpretations: The Presentation in the Temple, for instance, has been suggested.

20 **AN OLD BEGGAR · HEAD OF A WOMAN**

Pen. 150 × 115 mm. $5^{7}/_{8} \times 4^{1}/_{2}$ in. Formerly Warwick Collection, Warwick Castle.

One of the numerous sketches dating from the master's first years in Amsterdam.

21 **CRUCIFIXION**

Pen and bistre wash. 250 × 218 mm. $9^{7}/_{8} \times 8^{1}/_{2}$ in. Stockholm, Print Room.

This subject was frequently treated by Rembrandt. The rounded top of the sheet may justify the suggestion that this drawing was a preparatory study for a picture. It dates, at any rate, from a fairly advanced period; according to Valentiner, about 1645.

22 **FARMHOUSE WITH A LARGE TREE**

Pen and brush. 175 × 265 mm. $6^{7}/_{8} \times 10^{1}/_{2}$ in. Chatsworth, Collection of the Duke of Devonshire.

This shows Rembrandt's landscape drawing in its full maturity and mastery. It stands comparison with the etchings of 1641 (Hind).

23 **RECUMBENT LION**

Pen and brush. 138 × 207 mm. $5^{3}/_{8} \times 8^{1}/_{8}$ in. Paris, Musée du Louvre.

Rembrandt drew a whole series of lions. Numerous copies have been passed under his name. This drawing shows what an original is like. According to Lugt it dates from about 1640.

24 **SEATED NUDE**

Pen and brush. 292 × 195 mm. $11^{1}/_{2} \times 7^{5}/_{8}$ in. Rotterdam, Boymans Museum (Franz Koenigs Collection).

At the very end of his career as an etcher, Rembrandt executed some studies of the nude. This is a fine example of the few drawings which are more or less related to this series.

25 **WOMAN AT A WINDOW**

Pen and bistre wash. 295 × 164 mm. $11^{5}/_{8} \times 6^{1}/_{2}$ in. Paris, Musée du Louvre (de Rothschild Collection).

The drawing may well represent Hendrickje Stoffels. The technique may be compared with the studies of 1661 for *The Syndics of the Drapers' Guild*.

JAN LIEVENS

Born at Leyden in 1607; died at Amsterdam in 1674

Painter of historical subjects, portraits, genre and landscape; etcher and wood-engraver; pupil of Pieter Lastman; influenced at first by Rembrandt, who was his elder by a year. He then worked in England and at Antwerp, where he came under the influence of Van Dyck. His drawings consist chiefly of portraits, in which he sometimes attained monumental grandeur, and of landscapes, usually executed with a reed pen.

26 PORTRAIT OF JAN UYTENBOGAERT

Signed with the monogram JL and dated 1650. The name of the sitter on the back. Black chalk. 320×253 mm. 12 5/8×10 in. Amsterdam, Fodor Museum.

Uytenbogaert was the tax-collector of the town of Amsterdam. He is better known under the name of *The Gold-Weigher*, title of the Rembrandt etching of 1639.

GERRIT DOU

Born at Leyden in 1613; died there in 1675

Pupil of Rembrandt, whose development, however, increasingly diverged from that of his master. He finally became the leading genre painter of Leyden. The extraordinarily minute and detailed style of his paintings is not always apparent in the few drawings known to be by him.

27 OLD WOMAN WITH A MUFF

Signed: G.Dou. Black and red chalk. 168×130 mm. 6 5/8×5 1/8 in. London, British Museum.

This drawing shows Dou working in a manner not unlike that of the young Rembrandt.

PHILIPS DE KONINCK

Born at Amsterdam in 1619; died there in 1688

Painter, chiefly of landscapes. Some of his pictures showing wide stretches of countryside intersected by rivers are among the most splendid productions of seventeenth-century Dutch art. Though it is improbable that Koninck was Rembrandt's pupil, he certainly was under the great artist's influence.

28 LANDSCAPE IN GELDERLAND

Water-colour, heightened with white. 136×197 mm. 5 3/8×7 3/4 in. Haarlem, Teyler Museum.

Koninck's drawings, which are often coloured, are sometimes sketches in the proper sense of the term; others, as this one, are water-colours which seem like independently conceived small-scale masterpieces.

LAMBERT DOOMER

Born at Amsterdam in 1622 or 1623; died there in 1700

Pupil of Rembrandt. Few paintings by him are known. His reputation is based on the vigorous and sparingly-coloured drawings which he made during a journey through Germany, Switzerland, and France, and from which he borrowed his themes for later works.

29 THE TOWER OF THE "BELVEDERE" AT NIJMEGEN

Pen and wash in two colours. 238×357 mm. 9 3/8×14 in. Amsterdam, Rijks-Prentenkabinet.

Inscribed on the back: "*t belvedeer en de hoenderpoort te nijmegen*" (the Belvedere Tower and the gate known as the Hoenderpoort at Nijmegen). The tower still stands, occupying the site of the "Valkhof" (Falcon Court), Charlemagne's old hunting lodge.

GERBRAND VAN DEN EECKHOUT (?)

Born at Amsterdam in 1621; died there in 1674

Painter, draughtsman and etcher; pupil of Rembrandt. The distinction of Van den Eeckhout's art lies in the skill with which he employed a variety of techniques. Though he followed Rembrandt closely when drawing subjects which were similar to those of his master, he went his own way with the ones he selected himself.

30

BOY LEANING ON A CHAIR

Bistre wash. 182×147 mm. 7 1/8×5 3/4 in. Vienna, Albertina.

This drawing has a close affinity to another group of studies showing a boy in various positions, which were traditionally ascribed to Van den Eeckhout. The authorship of Nicolaes Maes has also been taken into consideration. The broad and sure touch even recalls that of Fragonard, who, it is known, studied drawings such as these.

NICOLAES MAES

Born at Dordrecht in 1632; died at Amsterdam in 1693

Portrait and genre painter; pupil of Rembrandt. In his second phase, his portraits follow the fashion of their time. As a draughtsman, Maes had won a wide reputation in his earliest days when Rembrandt's influence on him was at its strongest. The secret of the effect of various contrasting tones of red was well known to him, and we are therefore not surprised at his preference for red chalk.

31

SEATED GIRL

Red chalk, black chalk (for the background) and bistre wash. 144×140 mm. 5 5/8×5 1/2 in. Paris, Ecole des Beaux-Arts.

This is one of Maes' most striking studies. It dates from his best period which immediately followed the years of his apprenticeship.

AELBERT CUYP

Born at Dordrecht in 1620; died there in 1691

Landscape, animal and figure painter. Pupil of his father Jacob Gerritsz Cuyp. A remarkable draughtsman, both in the firm strokes of his outlines and in his gift for the composition of landscapes. He is fond of introducing a mustard-coloured wash into his landscapes which is easy to recognize.

32

DUTCH LANDSCAPE

Signed: A. Cuyp. Black chalk and grey wash for the foreground, different coloured chalks for the background. 174×245 mm. 6 7/8×9 5/8 in. London, British Museum.

There is an obvious affinity here with the drawings of Rembrandt, though no direct connection between the two masters can be established.

JAN VAN DE CAPPELLE

Born about 1624 at Amsterdam; died there in 1679

Painter of marine subjects and winter scenes. His wealth—he was the son of a colour manufacturer—enabled him to assemble a large collection of paintings and drawings, including several by Rembrandt and Simon de Vlieger; there are distinct traces in his work of the influence of both these artists.

33 GOLFERS ON THE ICE

Signed: J. v. Capel. Wash-drawing. 153×210 mm. $6 \times 8^1/_4$ in. Haarlem, Teyler Museum.

We have here one of the rare drawings which can be attributed with certainty to Van de Cappelle. It shows his fine sense of tone values.

ADRIAEN VAN OSTADE

Born at Haarlem in 1610; died there in 1684

Painter of genre subjects, portraits, and scenes of peasant life; a brillant etcher; pupil of Frans Hals. His versatility in the use of different techniques in his drawings is striking: he used pen, crayon and water-colours with equal facility. His aquarelles, to which he devoted special attention in his declining years, are so beautifully finished that they rival the effect of paintings in oil. The origin of many of his paintings and etchings can, however, clearly be traced from these masterly studies.

34 PEASANT FAMILY AT THE FIRESIDE

Crayon, pen and colour washes in brown and grey. 240×222 mm. $9^1/_2 \times 8^3/_4$ in.
Amsterdam, Rijks-Prentenkabinet.

A drawing made during the master's mature period, harmoniously combining the compact solidity of the foreground figures with the lightly-rendered objects in the background.

35 FARMYARD

Signed: A. v. Ostade 1673. Pen and water-colour. 236×209 mm. $9^1/_4 \times 8^1/_4$ in.
Amsterdam, Fodor Museum.

This peaceful domestic scene, a mother surrounded by her children at play, is typical of Ostade's work.

AERT VAN DER NEER

Probably born at Amsterdam in 1603 or 1604; died there in 1677

This artist probably studied under the brothers Camphuysen at Gorkum. His favourite subjects were moonlight and snow. His pictures have a delicate tone and breathe an atmosphere of serene tranquillity. Another favourite subject was a fire at night. The few drawings known to be by him are done with an admirably free brush-stroke.

36 MOONLIGHT RIVER-SCENE

Signed: AV DN. Bistre wash, heightened with white on blue paper. 215×386 mm. $8^3/_8 \times 15^1/_4$ in. The Hague, Frits Lugt Collection.

This masterly drawing made during Van der Neer's mature period establishes him as an artist of truly poetic feeling.

NICOLAES BERCHEM

Born at Haarlem in 1620; died at Amsterdam in 1683

Landscape, animal and figure painter; etcher. Pupil of his father Pieter Claesz Berchem, of Nicolaes Moeyaert, Pieter de Grebber and Jan Wils. He travelled in Italy. A brilliant technique with a pointed brush enabled Berchem to bring out particularly well the effects of sunlight in his drawings.

37 SHEPHERDS AT A FOUNTAIN

Signed: Berchem f. 1657. Pen and bistre wash. On a mount stamped by Glomy. 285×373 mm. $11^1/_4 \times 14^3/_4$ in. Paris, Petit Palais (Dutuit Collection).

This drawing is a perfect example of the calculated light effects which were the particular aim of the second generation of seventeenth-century painters.

QUIRINGH GERRITSZ VAN BREKELENCAM

Born at Zwammerdam in 1620; died at Leyden in 1668

Painter of genre scenes, and especially those of middle-class life. His drawings are very rare.

38 A WOMAN READING THE BIBLE

Black chalk (crayon?). 235×173 mm. $9^1/_4 \times 6^3/_4$ in. Copenhagen, Print Room.

This drawing has hitherto been classified as anonymous. The attribution here made to Brekelencam is founded on the strong resemblance of the subject to figures in his paintings. Another figure of a seated woman is sketched on the back.

GABRIEL METSU

Born at Leyden in 1629; died at Amsterdam in 1667

Perhaps a pupil of Gerrit Dou whose style he followed, though he did not acquire his minuteness of detail. A genre painter of whom only a few drawings are known.

39 CAVALIER HOLDING A GUN

Black chalk, heightened with white, on dark paper. 302×200 mm. $11^7/_8 \times 7^7/_8$ in. Haarlem, Teyler Museum.

The drawing is catalogued under the name of Gerard Terborch the Younger. The attribution to Metsu may seem rash, in view of the absence of reliable sources of comparison. It is here suggested because of the strong resemblance of the figure to those in Metsu's paintings, especially as regards the type of the features (cf. Plate 41).

WILLEM KALF

Born at Amsterdam in 1622; died there in 1693

Painter of still lifes and interiors. Pupil of Hendrik Gerritsz Pot. The artist lived for some time in Paris. He reached a high perfection in rendering the texture and surface of objects in his still life pictures. Very few drawings by him are known to us.

40 STILL LIFE

Signed on the back: Kalf. Pen. 180×144 mm. 7 1/8×5 5/8 in. The Hague, Frits Lugt Collection.

It is impossible to decide from the character of the drawing whether it is a preparatory study for a painting or a drawing done after a finished picture.

GABRIEL METSU

(For biographical note see page XXIII)

41 WOMAN WASHING HER HANDS

Black chalk, heightened with white, on greyish paper. 250×150 mm. 9 7/8×5 7/8 in. Frankfort-on-Main, Städelsches Kunstinstitut.

The traditional ascription of this sheet to Terborch—our reproduction also still bears his name—is in need of revision. Shortly before the publication of this volume it became clear that this is a preparatory study for one of the three figures in a once famous painting by Gabriel Metsu which formerly was in the collection of the Baron de Rothschild at Frankfort. The drawing thus constitutes another key to our knowledge of Metsu's style of drawing (see page XXIII).

ADRIAEN VAN DE VELDE

Born at Amsterdam in 1636; died there in 1672

Animal, landscape and figure painter; etcher. Pupil of his father Willem van de Velde the Elder, and of Jan Wijnants. He probably travelled in Italy. During his short life, Adriaen van de Velde painted a series of pictures which we admire because of the masterly technique and the feeling for clear-cut classic forms. His numerous drawings include pen and brush studies, some roughly sketched, others highly finished; and figure studies in red chalk.

42 STUDY OF A RECLINING SHEPHERD

Signed: A. v. d. Velde f. Crayon and red chalk heightened with white. 200×292 mm. 7 7/8×11 1/2 in. Amsterdam, Rijks-Prentenkabinet.

The drawing shows the shepherd in two positions. The completed figure can be seen in a picture in the Museum at Karlsruhe and a combination of both poses in a drawing in red chalk of a sleeping shepherd in the Musée Condé at Chantilly.

JAN VERMEER VAN DELFT (?)

Born at Delft in 1632; died there in 1675

The master of the Delft school of painting. Pupil of Carel Fabritius. Vermeer painted figures, interiors, and views of towns. He knew how to achieve wonderful light effects and convey a sensation of absolute stillness and concentration. To date, there have been hardly any drawings that could be ascribed to him with certainty.

43 GIRL ASLEEP UNDER A TREE

Red chalk on light brown paper. 395×445 mm. 15 1/2×17 1/2 in.
Amsterdam, Private Collection.

This drawing recalls the earliest pictures Vermeer is known to have painted.

ADRIAEN VAN DE VELDE

(For biographical note see page XXIV)

44 GRAZING ANIMALS IN A FOREST CLEARING

Black chalk, pen with wash and bistre. 138×202 mm. 5 3/8×8 in. Paris, Ecole des Beaux-Arts.

The same composition, in reverse, is seen in two drawings in the Fodor Museum, Amsterdam and in the Louvre, Paris.

WILLEM VAN DE VELDE THE YOUNGER

Born at Leyden in 1633; died in London in 1707

Pupil of his father Willem van de Velde the Elder, and of Simon de Vlieger. He was a marine painter and carried out the work of his father who specialized in pictures of naval battles between the Dutch and the English. Shipping was also the favourite subject in his numerous drawings, treated, in turn, as large-scale composition, a spirited sketch, or simply as a "portrait" of a ship.

45 VESSELS IN A CALM

Pen and wash. 179×286 mm. 7×11 1/4 in. Present ownership unknown.

The drawings of Van de Velde are sometimes documentary, sometimes poetic. This example illustrates the latter quality.

JAN DE BRAY

Born at Haarlem about 1627; died there in 1697

Painter of religious and secular subjects and of portraits. Pupil of his father, Salomon de Bray. He was a good draughtsman and etcher; several fine portraits by him are known. His drawings are in various techniques, and characterized by precise and careful execution. The date is frequently added to the signature.

46 PORTRAIT OF A GIRL

Dated: 1663 $\frac{7}{10}$. Black and red chalk. 186×151 mm. $7^3/_8$×6 in.
Amsterdam, Chr. P. van Eeghen Collection.

The measured use of red chalk adds greatly to the charm of this typically Dutch drawing.

CASPAR NETSCHER

Born at Heidelberg in 1639; died at The Hague in 1684

Painter of portraits, genre, and mythological subjects. Pupil of Hendrick Coster, and of Gerard Terborch the Younger. Netscher spent some time in France and his pictures clearly show the influence of French painting. In some of his drawings he attains striking effects with his flowing and facile brush-strokes.

47 YOUNG MAN PONDERING OVER A LETTER

Brush-drawing and wash. 152×122 mm. 6×$4^3/_4$ in. London, British Museum.

Study for the painting of 1665 at Dresden. There was formerly an inscription on the back indicating that the drawing had been a study for a picture painted in 1664, and naming also its price.

JACOB VAN RUISDAEL

Born at Haarlem in 1628 or 1629; died there in 1682

Pupil of his father and perhaps of his uncle, Salomon van Ruisdael. Landscape and marine painter in the grand manner whose scenery is dramatic rather than lyrical. Ruisdael also worked as an etcher and draughtsman. His drawings are executed in black chalk and with the brush. Their effect lies in the accumulation of many small strokes with hardly distinguishable changes in accent which combine into a harmonious whole.

48 THE JEWISH CEMETERY AT OUDERKERK

Signed: Ruisdael f. Black chalk and wash. 190×275 mm. $7^1/_2$×$10^7/_8$ in.
Haarlem, Teyler Museum.

This drawing was one of a pair, both at Haarlem. There is a second pair of drawings, somewhat similar, which show other views of the same cemetery and can be traced through various auctions in the nineteenth and twentieth centuries; these appear, however, to have been only sketched in by Ruisdael, and finished by Dirk Dalens. The drawing at Haarlem is the inspiration of the painting in the Detroit Museum; also of that at Dresden, which inspired Goethe's reflections on "*Ruisdael als Dichter*" (Ruisdael as Poet).

49 DUNES

Black chalk, grey and white wash, on greyish paper. 230×378 mm. 9×$14^7/_8$ in.
Berlin, Kupferstichkabinett.

The various pictures by Ruisdael of the Dutch beaches at different seasons of the year are among his finest works. A drawing like this shows how the artist steeped himself in the life of nature.

JAN STEEN

Born at Leyden about 1626; died there in 1679

Genre painter. Pupil of Nicolaus Knüpfer, and Jan van Goyen, whose daughter he married. Very few drawings can definitely be ascribed to him, but a resemblance can be found between certain drawings and his pictures. Unlike Adriaen van Ostade, Jan Steen apparently never really cultivated the art of drawing.

50 RUSTIC HOLIDAY

Signed: J. Steen. Crayon, pen, brush and bistre wash. 328×449 mm. $12^{7}/_{8} \times 17^{5}/_{8}$ in. Berlin, Kupferstichkabinett.

Jan Steen's drawings are but outlines of compositions and of motions. They are rapidly sketched and without pretensions to any great artistic quality. This is a preliminary study for a picture of which only the description is known to us.

JAN VAN DER HEYDEN

Born at Gorkum in 1637; died at Amsterdam in 1712

Painter, engraver and draughtsman. Possibly a pupil of Jan van der Ulft. He painted landscapes and views of towns, and was much interested in architecture. Some of his carefully executed drawings are preparatory studies for his engravings.

51 STUDIES OF FIREMEN AT WORK

Crayon. 190×307 mm. $7^{1}/_{2} \times 12^{1}/_{8}$ in. Amsterdam, Rijks-Prentenkabinet.

Jan van der Heyden combined the rôles of artist and technician. He was the owner of a factory producing fire-fighting apparatuses and considerably improved the efficiency of the equipment by introducing the pipe system. To make known this invention he wrote and published a book in 1690, and illustrated it with his own engravings. This drawing is a first study for figures which, however, were not repeated exactly in his final compositions.—The firemen in a print by Van der Heyden showing a conflagration which occurred in 1684 resemble those seen here; this suggests that the drawing was made at about the time of the catastrophe in question.

MEINDERT HOBBEMA

Born at Amsterdam in 1638; died there in 1709

The last great landscape painter of seventeenth-century Holland. Pupil of Jacob van Ruisdael. Hobbema's drawings so much resemble those of his teacher that it is often difficult to decide on the authorship.

52 WATERMILL IN GELDERLAND

Signed on the back: M. Hobbema f. 166· Black chalk and wash. 182×295 mm. $7^{1}/_{8} \times 11^{5}/_{8}$ in. Haarlem, Teyler Museum.

The watermill is a favourite subject with both Ruisdael and Hobbema. An inscription on the back of this drawing and the similarity to a signed painting make it possible to accept the traditional attribution.

VALENTIN KLOTZ

Active between 1669 and 1697

An engineer who made topographical drawings in the southern part of what is now the Netherlands. They are duly provided with dates and indications of place, and relate partly to the campaigns of William III against Louis XIV. Klotz' work is easily confused with the drawings of Josua de Grave.

53 VIEW IN BERGEN OP ZOOM

Pen and wash. 200×322 mm. $7^7/_8 \times 12^3/_4$ in. Haarlem, Teyler Museum. Inscribed: "Tot Bergem op den Zoom de $\frac{3\text{ m}}{9\text{ d}}$ 1672."

JAN DE BISSCHOP

Born at Amsterdam in 1628; died at The Hague in 1671

Jan de Bisschop, known as Episcopius, seems to have been a man of learning who had a fine understanding of drawing. His studies bear witness to the fact. They consist of renderings of various works of art, of landscapes, and impressions of his travels to Italy. Some of his drawings are so masterly as to approach in quality those of Rembrandt.

54 THE WALLS OF DELFT AND THE "KOLK"

Pencil, pen and brush, with "Bisschop ink" wash. 94×158 mm. $3^3/_4 \times 6^1/_4$ in. Amsterdam, Fodor Museum.

The same tower on which the sunlight here is falling stands in the middle distance of the famous *View of Delft* by Jan Vermeer. This drawing seems to reflect some of the magic light effect of that well-known masterpiece.

CONSTANTIN HUYGENS

Born at The Hague in 1628; died there in 1697

The son of the well-known poet of the same name; man of letters; secretary to the Prince of Orange; and an art lover like his father. If he did not possess his father's erudition and literary talent, he excelled him as a draughtsman. Best known are his travel impressions, drawn with much wit and spirit.

55 VIEW OF THE COURTYARD OF THE OLD CASTLE OF DIEREN (?)

Pen. 141×202 mm. $5^1/_2 \times 8$ in. Amsterdam, Rijks-Prentenkabinet. Inscribed: "Dieren. 2. Nov. 1678"; on the back: "dieren 8. octob. 1678 2. Nov. 1678."

It is possible to correlate many of Huygens' drawings with the text of his travel diaries, or rather his notes on army campaigns; this cannot be done here, since the diary for 1678 ends in August. It is, however, quite possible that the artist was in Dieren in November for it was one of the favourite residences of Prince William III.

HERMAN SAFTLEVEN

Born at Rotterdam in 1609; died at Utrecht in 1685

Landscape and animal painter. Pupil of his father, Herman Saftleven, of Jan van Goyen and of his brother, Cornelis Saftleven. He was a prolific draughtsman; his fine series of topographical drawings and views of the Rhineland is quite well known. Most of his studies of flowers and plants, however, are hitherto unpublished, though they include some of his best works.

56 CACTUS IN FLOWER

Water-colour. 355×257 mm. 14×10 1/8 in. Amsterdam, Rijks-Prentenkabinet.

This drawing is mentioned among those which the collector Röver acquired from the estate of Agneta Block, a lady of great wealth and culture, who grew many rare plants at her country place, which she had drawn by various artists.

Photographs:

Bern. F. Eilers, Amsterdam: 36, 40. – Gemeente Musea, Amsterdam: 11, 26, 35. – Lichtbeelden-Instituut, Amsterdam: 7a, 24. – Rijksmuseum, Amsterdam: 8, 9, 12, 15, 17b, 29, 34, 42, 54, 55, 56. – A. Frequin, The Hague: 4, 43, 46. – British Museum, London: 27. – Archives photographiques, Paris: 31. – J. E. Bulloz, Paris: 23. – A. Giraudon, Paris: 44. – Nationalmusei, Stockholm: 21. – Paul Frankenstein, Vienna: 30.

PLATES

HENDRICK GOLTZIUS

1

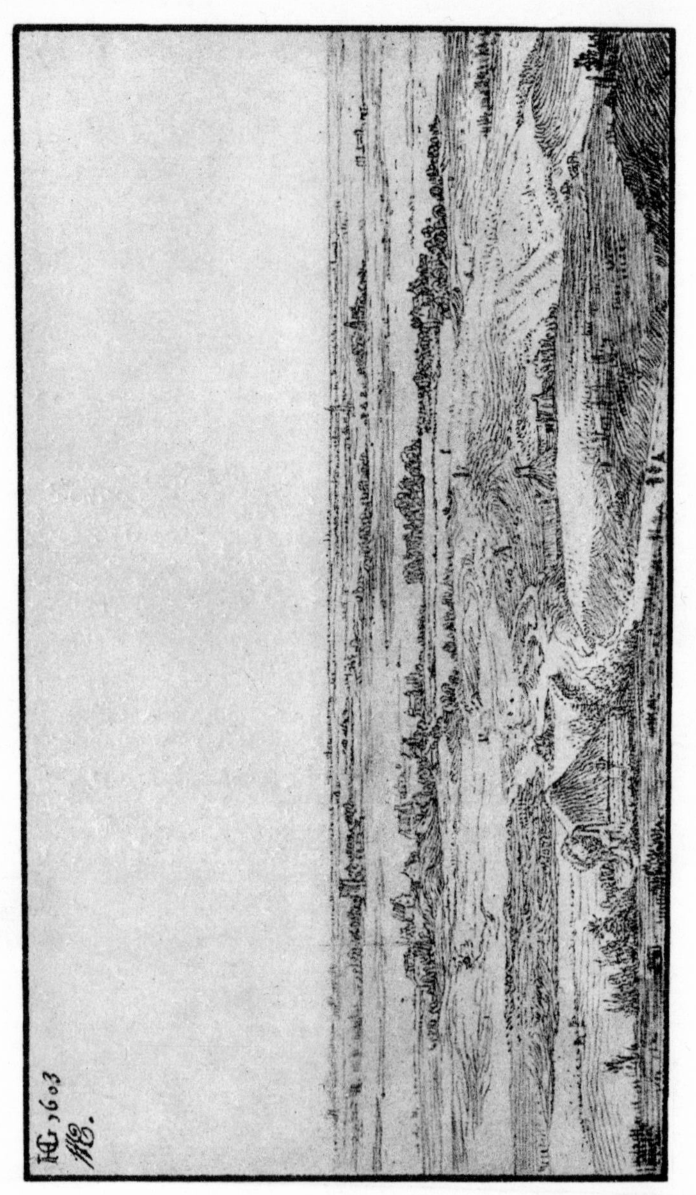

HENDRICK GOLTZIUS

ABRAHAM BLOEMAERT

JACQUES DE GHEYN

JACQUES DE GHEYN

REMBRANDT

6

JACQUES DE GHEYN

HENDRICK GOLTZIUS

HENDRICK AVERCAMP

HENDRICK AVERCAMP

ROELANT SAVERY

10

PIETER SAENREDAM

WILLEM PIETERSZ BUYTEWECH (?)

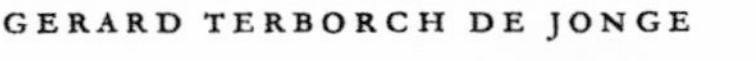

GERARD TERBORCH DE JONGE

JAN VAN GOYEN

SIMON DE VLIEGER

FRANS HALS

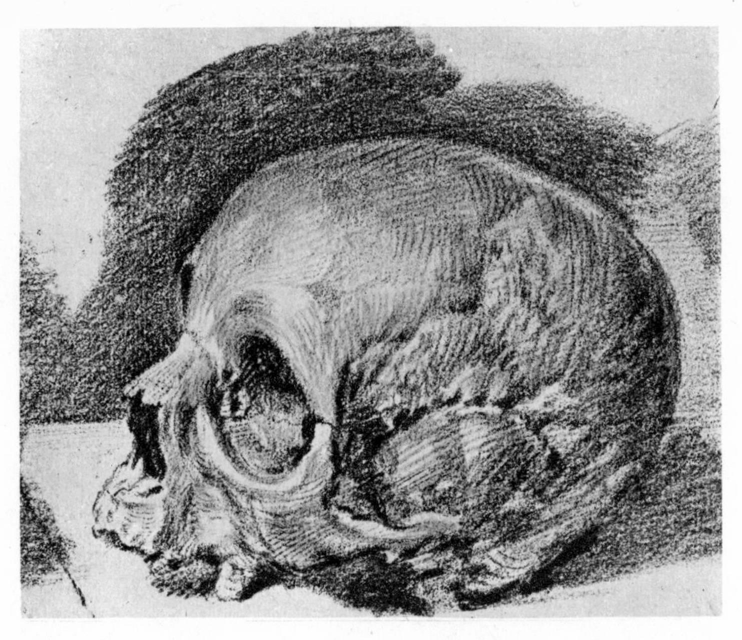

CORNELIS VISSCHER

BARTHOLOMEUS BREENBERGH

REMBRANDT

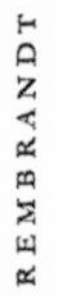

REMBRANDT

REMBRANDT

REMBRANDT

REMBRANDT

REMBRANDT

REMBRANDT

24

REMBRANDT

JAN LIVENS

GERRIT DOU

PHILIPS DE KONINCK

LAMBERT DOOMER

GERBRAND VAN DEN EECKHOUT (?)

NICOLAES MAES

AELBERT CUYP

JAN VAN DE CAPPELLE

ADRIAEN VAN OSTADE

ADRIAEN VAN OSTADE

AERT VAN DER NEER

NICOLAES BERCHEM

QUIRINGH GERRITSZ VAN BREKELENCAM

GABRIEL METSU

WILLEM KALF

GERARD TERBORCH DE JONGE

ADRIAEN VAN DE VELDE

JAN VERMEER VAN DELFT (?)

ADRIAEN VAN DE VELDE

WILLEM VAN DE VELDE DE JONGE

JAN DE BRAY

CASPAR NETSCHER

JACOB VAN RUISDAEL

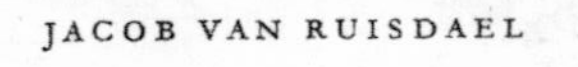

JACOB VAN RUISDAEL

JAN STEEN

JAN VAN DER HEYDEN

MEINDERT HOBBEMA

VALENTIN KLOTZ

JAN DE BISSCHOP

CONSTANTIN HUYGENS

HERMAN SAFTLEVEN